breaking bread together:
families growing in the
practice of Eucharist

by Rick Morley

This book is presented to:

_____

Presented by:

_____

On the occasion of:

_____

Date:

_____

Breaking Bread Together: Families Growing in the Practice of Eucharist
Written and Illustrated by Rick Morley

All liturgical quotes are from The Book of Common Prayer, 1979.

ISBN 10: 0985462906
ISBN 13: 978-0-9854629-0-1

This book is dedicated to
my girls, Zoë and Mattie.

The liturgical selections in Part Two are from The Book of Common Prayer, 1979, of The Episcopal Church. If these prayers are different from your tradition, please substitute or amend them to be the most appropriate for your family's use.

Part One
The Stories

Part Two
Things to Know and Learn

Part One

The Feeding of the Multitudes
John 6:1-13

One day a huge crowd came to hear Jesus talk about the amazing power of God's love.

Thousands showed up. Adults, teenagers, and children all wanted to see Jesus. Jesus led them all up to the top of a high mountain, and he talked to them all day long about how much God loves us.

There was a problem though.

It got late and the people began to get hungry for dinner. On the top of the mountain there were no stores, and certainly no restaurants.

There was practically nothing to eat.

And even though the people loved listening to Jesus…their bellies started to rumble. And the littlest kids…well, they started to fuss a bit.

Jesus asked his disciples, "Where are we going to get bread for all of these people to eat?"

The disciples…had no idea.

After a lot of thinking, a disciple came to Jesus and said, "You know, there's a little boy over there who has two fish and five loaves of bread…but, of course there's no way this little bit of food is going to feed everyone!"

Jesus told the disciples to bring him the little bit of food from the boy, and to tell people to sit down and get ready to eat.

Jesus **took** the loaves of bread, **gave thanks** to God, **broke** the bread, and **gave** the fish and bread out to the people.

He asked the disciples to help him hand out all the food.

Everyone in the humongous crowd ate…until they were full! Everyone had as much food as they wanted!

And when it was over the crumbs of bread and leftover bits of fish filled twelve baskets to the brim.

What had happened?

Jesus had performed a miracle.

He turned a little bit of food, into more than enough food. And everyone thanked God for what they had seen, and for what they have eaten.

The Last Supper

Matthew 26:24-25
Mark 14:18-21
Luke 22:21-23

A couple of years later—on the night before Jesus died—he sat down and had a meal with his disciples. Everyone had gathered around a big table in a big room in the big city of Jerusalem.

They sang songs, they told stories, and they enjoyed each other's company. They talked about how God always helps us when we need it the most.

Then, just before supper was served, Jesus **took** some bread, he **gave thanks** to God, he **broke** the bread and he **gave** it to his disciples.

Jesus said, "Take, eat. This is my body which is given for you. Do this for the remembrance of me."

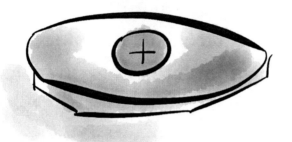

After supper, Jesus **took** a cup of wine, he **gave thanks** to God, and he **gave** it to his disciples.

He said, "Take this, all of you, and drink it. This is my blood of the new covenant which is given for you, and for many, for the forgiveness of sins. Do this as often as you drink it for the remembrance of me."

We call this meal "The Last Supper."

This meal was very special. It was the meal that showed Jesus' friends and disciples how much he loves all of us.

The Walk to Emmaus

Luke 24:13-24

A few days later, on the first Easter day, two of the disciples went on a journey from Jerusalem to a village called Emmaus. They knew that Jesus had died, and so they were very, very sad.

There were rumors that Jesus had risen from the dead that very morning...but they didn't think that was possible.

Along the way to Emmaus they ran into another man—a stranger—who was going in the same direction. They all started walking together.

As they were walking, the two disciples were telling the stranger all about Jesus, about his stories of the amazing power of God's love, and about his death on the cross. They told him how sad they were, and about how much they loved Jesus.

When they got to Emmaus the stranger wanted to keep walking, but the disciples asked him to stay with them and eat, because it was getting late.

So the stranger sat down with them, and he **took** a loaf of bread, he **gave thanks** to God, he **broke** the bread, and he **gave** it to the two disciples.

As soon as the stranger broke the bread, the disciples knew that it wasn't a stranger after all! It was Jesus! It was Easter day, and Jesus had really risen!

Even though it was very late, the disciples hurried back to Jerusalem to tell the other disciples that they had seen Jesus, and that even though they didn't recognize him at first, they had recognized him in the breaking of the bread.

In Church

When we go to church today there are sometimes huge crowds of adults, teenagers, and children present—just like on the mountaintop.

And other times there's just a few people there—like on the road to Emmaus.

At church we read lessons from the Bible and we hear a sermon which reminds us about the amazing power of God's love.

We pray. We sing songs.

And then we set the table—the Altar—for Eucharist. On the Altar we put bread and wine, and we pray, giving thanks to God for all the things that God has given us.

We pray that God would come to us and make the bread and wine holy.

Then the bread is broken, and it's time to receive the Eucharist.

The word "holy" means "special"
or "set apart."

The word "Eucharist" means
"thanksgiving."

Do you notice what happens?

We **take** the bread and wine, we **give thanks** to God, we **break** the bread, and we **give** the bread and wine to God's people.

Does that sound familiar?!

It's what Jesus did on the mountaintop, the Last Supper, and on the road to Emmaus.

We celebrate the Eucharist this way because it's what Jesus taught us to do.

And in the Eucharist we remember Jesus, we recognize him in the breaking of the bread, and we celebrate the amazing power of God's love for us all.

Part Two

The Sursum Corda

"Sursum Corda" literally means "hearts up!" or "Lift up your hearts." This call-and-response is the way that a Eucharistic prayer typically begins.

The Lord be with you.
And also with you.
Lift up your hearts.
We lift them to the Lord.
Let us give thanks to the Lord our God.
It is right to give him thanks and praise.

The Sanctus

This is the song that we hear the angels sing in heaven in various places of the Bible. Oftentimes in the Eucharistic prayer this hymn is sung by the whole congregation.

Holy, Holy, Holy Lord, God of power and might, heaven and earth are full of your glory.
  Hosanna in the highest.
Blessed is he who comes in the name of the Lord.
  Hosanna in the highest.

The Memorial Acclamation

A statement of the mystery of our faith.

Therefore we proclaim the mystery of faith:
Christ has died,
Christ is risen,
Christ will come again.

Or,

Therefore, according to his command, O Father,
We remember his death,
We proclaim his resurrection,
We await his coming in glory.

The Lord's Prayer

The prayer that Jesus taught his disciples.

Our Father, who art in heaven,
   hallowed be thy Name,
   thy kingdom come,
   thy will be done,
     on earth as it is in heaven.
Give us this day our daily bread.
And forgive us our trespasses,
   as we forgive those
     who trespass against us.
And lead us not into temptation,
   but deliver us from evil.
For thine is the kingdom,
   and the power, and the glory,
   for ever and ever. Amen.

The Great Amen.

At the end of the Eucharistic Prayer we all say "Amen!" Amen literally means "so be it." It's important that we all say, or sing, "amen" together.

...By him and with him and in him, in the unity of the Holy Spirit, all honor and glory is yours Almighty Father, now and forever!
Amen!

The Fraction Anthem

*What we say, or sing, after the breaking of the bread.
This verse is from 1 Corinthians 5:17. (During the
season of Lent we leave the "alleluia's" out.)*

[Alleluia.] Christ our Passover is sacrificed for us;
Therefore let us keep the feast. [Alleluia.]

Receiving the Eucharist

*Come forward, and stand or kneel, with your hands
extended, palms up and flat and wide open, with the
right hand crossed over the left hand. After receiving
the bread and the wine, we say "Amen."*

The Body of Christ, the bread of heaven.
Amen.

The Blood of Christ, the cup of salvation.
Amen.

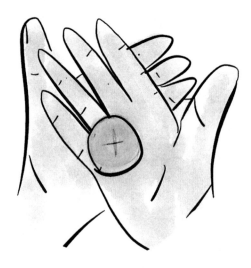

Post-Communion Prayer

After everyone receives Communion, we all pray together.

Let us pray.
Eternal God, heavenly Father, you have graciously accepted us as living members of your Son our Savior Jesus Christ, and you have fed us with spiritual food in the Sacrament of his Body and Blood. Send us now into the world in peace, and grant us strength and courage to love and serve you with gladness and singleness of heart; through Christ our Lord. Amen.

CPSIA information can be obtained at www.ICGtesting.com
Printed in the USA
LVOW05s2107020514

384218LV00001B/290/P